Collection of Poems

By
Esmeralda

Collection of Poems

Author: Esmeralda

Copyright © Esmeralda (2025)

The right of Esmeralda to be identified as author of this work has been asserted by the author in accordance with section 77 and 78 of the Copyright, Designs and Patents Act 1988.

First Published in 2025

ISBN 978-1-83538-719-1 (Paperback)
    978-1-83538-746-7 (Hardback)
    978-1-83538-720-7 (E-Book)

Book cover design and Book layout by:
    White Magic Studios
    www.whitemagicstudios.co.uk

Published by:
    Maple Publishers
    Fairbourne Drive, Atterbury,
    Milton Keynes,
    MK10 9RG, UK
    www.maplepublishers.com

A CIP catalogue record for this title is available from the British Library.

All rights reserved. No part of this book may be reproduced or translated by any form or by any means, electronic or mechanical, including photocopying, recording or by any information storage and retrieval system without written permission from the author.

The book is a work of fiction. Unless otherwise indicated, all the names, characters, places and incidents are either the product of the author's imagination or used in a fictitious manner. Any resemblance to actual people living or dead, events or locales is entirely coincidental, and the Publisher hereby disclaims any responsibility for them.

Contents

Part 1

- Otto 6
- He 8
- Absent 9
- Hiding 10
- Wet 11
- Turkey After The Quake 12
- Turkey After the Quake 2 14
- The First Day 16
- Nameless 18
- Piazza 20
- Oliver 21
- Listening to Orb 23
- Waiting 24
- The Last Stop 26
- Journey 28

Part 2

- A New War 30
- Fear 31
- Dereliction 32
- Flakes 34
- The Children 35
- Poppy Fields 36
- Rain 37

Part 3

- Sleepless 39
- Play 41
- Tomorrow 42
- Silent Fugue 43
- The Couple 44
- Only a Child Could Dream 46

Part 1

Otto

An elderly gent
White beard and hair
Suited in pale blue pinstripe
Announces his presence to the dancefloor

The audience stares in amazement
The aim to astonish never fails.

She slides gently alongside
Inhabiting his space
Demonstrating an idea of herself
As a young girl
With astounding attention to detail
Pearls adorn a slender neck
The simple dress is just enough

Together they reimagine youth
Silent timepieces gliding
Across the dancefloor
They weave mazes
No one can break the spell

Reaching floating point with
The music inside them
Spinning zones of gentle energy
As
The fragile architecture
Of their bodies
Unveils a dream.

He

He carries things
Cap, socks, neatly laid out across
Open palms with utmost care
As if they hold a fragility known
Only to him
And he walks in slow silence
As if on eggshells

His world is paced, peaceful, content

While all around they race
Into each new day
And back again
Desultory then
Exhausted
Searching and striving

Set on repeat.

Absent

His absence was louder
Than the hissing rain
That sliced the silence
And tapped on windowpanes
Louder, faster
More insistent
With every passing second

The hammer of her heartbeat
Set cogs of memory moving

Remembering
Was a dull ache
That needed to be gone

Her thoughts clawed
At the image of him
Dragging the past back to life

Like echo chambers after a scream.

Hiding

A secret has no sound
It hides in the shadows
In the private corners of your mind
Like a dissolute bluebottle
Waiting
To be set free
And fly away.

The silence of a secret moves
Like a cloud covering
Growing
Thick and heavy with
Unspoken words

Until a scream
Slices the silence and
Suddenly with a hiss
It is gone.

Wet

Rain
Drums on a tin roof
Aloof and
Happily wet with
Bounce and splatter it
Spills from the hills
Creating fault lines
Running soggy like deep glue
Making a dissolute land
A floating point as
Silence settles
Absorbing sound

The natural world emits a power
So intricate
Everything in nature rearranges itself
Eventually

Birds begin their chorus as
A delicate network of song
Becomes the music inside us.

Turkey After The Quake

A Child

Standing in a broken doorway, hesitant
The naivety of not knowing chafes
Tentatively she enters the fractured room
Clinging to hope
A rope swings
In and out as
She lunges
Trying desperately to stop it
Slipping away

Yesterday's smoke hangs in the air
Silence drips thick and heavy
Memories of music echo
A rhythmic beat
Pulsating like a promise

Remembering is slow

With imaginary wanderings
Words knock against walls

Hiding silently and oh so still
She listens
To the sound of ants walking
Then once again the hiss of silence

Fear bends seconds intolerably
She has the sense of being stuck
Inside an inescapable loop of time

Outside she hears the music of the wind
While a secret gnaws at her brain
A reminder
It can be easier to let bad things happen
So she hides there
Remembering
Aching to forget.

Turkey After the Quake 2

Crouching under a bed
Waiting
For the earth to become still
A child breathes fast and shallow
Alive, afraid, exhausted until
Evening announced its presence.

Shadows push
Against one another
Lying in wait
Ready to molest
As all around the night erupts
Enhanced by the moon
As it drops its bone white light
Across the wall.

The wind sighs
Then silence
He focused on the shadows
Friends now

Sleep came easily as
Beneath the skin of a dream
The young child slept.

The First Day

My first day at school I met the tree
Whose leaves smelled divine
Ribbed veins rubbed with soil
Made an imprint on my little hand

The tree was my friend
The children were not
My teacher was not

I hid in the cloakroom at playtime
So the boy could not spin me around
Dropping me onto hard tarmac
Grazing knees

Ten years of school never changed
I was friends with the grass on the field
And with the tree whose leaves smelled divine
With ribbed veins that made an imprint
On the back of my hand

The leaf print lasted all day.

At home time my mum made me
Wash it away.

Nameless

In a city without a name
At an unknown place
A child waited to be born
And thaw frozen time

The child fumbled in the womb
Mumbled bubbles as
The waiting grew impatient

Bed sheets rumpled like old skin
Silence pressed against walls
Ready to absorb sound

Ceiling fan blades sliced the air
Dust motes danced and
As dark became light
The waiting ended

Her face stretched into caricatures of pain
That signaled beginnings not endings
The womans deep and sonorous cry
Zeroed in pitch perfect and
With a power so intricate
A child was born.

Piazza

Streaming light
Scorches the Piazza

Upon the grass
A green pile carpet
We lounge
Bronze skin burning
A welcome breeze blowing

Pigeons strut like punks
Their regalia of colour
Purple black
Orange hair bright

And green the grass
Where a busker sits
Strumming
The hot sun streaming

Oliver

Battered and bruised we were
Too exhausted to cry
His blood stained body lay
Limp on mine

His head on my shoulder
I looked into those wide
Bewildered eyes
Trying to focus their terror
In the silence healing our wounds
And I loved him
My new life

I hold him close
Nibble his cheek
This satin skin soft

I want to hold him
For all his tomorrows

A little sob
He sighs asleep

I leave this part of me
To the care of the moon
As she whispers her promises
And fills the room
With the blue light
Of her glow.

Listening to Orb

I turn on the music and
Listen to Orb
I look across at the mountain of dishes
And look away

I glance outside at the existence of things
And feel my life is filling up nicely

Time reduces it
Making it smaller
The world is getting bigger
And where are we?

Sat inside our plastic bubbles
Waiting for time to stop.

Waiting

A bus station
Cold and wet

Silent Sunday people filter
Through draughty stone and steel
Each one to a separate but
Similar destination

The absent father
Arms outstretched
Cigarette hanging from limp lips
An aperitif anticipating
Rare delicacies in his loveless void

A teenage raver
Slowly sobering
Leaning limp over a half drunk
Bottle of milk
His skull still full
Of acid and E's
Anticipating the next rave

A bus driver
Cup of tepid tea slopping
Onto polished shoes

He mounts his cabin
Taps in numbers
For the computer to assess

Silent passengers board
And move on.

The Last Stop

You passed this way
Only once
And even then
Only in my dreams passionate fantasy
An episode that many seldom know
Unless by concession

But this much was sure
You passed my way
And stayed over a while
The last stop on a tortured journey
And you favoured me with your presence

You engraved your message upon my heart
Like the tattoo on your arm
Blue now and cold

You surrendered yourself to the elements
The black gulls didn't stand a chance
You'd already cleaned yourself out

You might have passed this way only once
But only by concession.

Journey

I am inhabited by a scream
A thirsty noise seeking refuge in stillness
Like a black hole it hides inside itself

And with each new blood throb
Pulsating through veins
I feel this scream drinking up my sense

And I become like shed skin
Crumpled and torn

In the stillborn silence
When the coldness has gone
A splinter of light cracks the black

As a fetus begins its blood rush
To the brain
And the silence is over

The stillness has gone
Falling into the light
We become whole again.

Part 2

A New War

His blood
Their child
A million miles from safety sensing
Where the next bomb will land and
Blow the blue from the sky
The air from their lungs

Feeling his way into the dust filled darkness
Going blind across acres of rubble
Deaf with the last hole
Their home
A new landscape

Fear

A trickle of fear
Tickles like a feather. Yet
Heavy as rainfall
Saturates

Bombed out buildings
Where dust settles
Everything coated white
Except for the blood
Pooling around
Victims on the ground

The massacre continues as
Leaders look on
Afraid of upsetting
The balance of evil.

Dereliction

I walked slowly through the open door
Senses super alert
The keyhole stared back at me

The air was silent and still
But for a single light bulb
Buzzing insistently above

The room was a place where aged flies
Go to die
Stacked everywhere in small mounds

Outside I heard the sound of crows
That no one sees at night
Their caw caw caw grating through
Soupy blackness

I felt fear
A wet smudge of grey black
A tickle
Light as a feather
This must be how a shadow feels

I swallowed thickly at the sound of rain
That looked like melting silver and
Dripped down window panes

A thousand tears.

Flakes

The sky is grey
Ruins lie barren and cold
Snow flakes create
A spellbinding ballet of white

In the distance children scream
Tiny fragments of joy
A gale of laughter
A spinning kaleidoscope
Of hope
In a desolate land.

The Children

Remember the dance they made
Dipping then reaching
For the sky
As if they might fly
Away

They played amidst ruins
Of a lost land
Where spiders webs glimmered
Like strands of their hair

Hand in hand
They skipped and ran
Through broken buildings
Bright cries ringing

In a place of desolation
And despair
They create dreams.

Poppy Fields

Like poppy fields
Their bodies lie
Saturated
Counting no more tomorrows

Their opium days began
With a song of freedom
But it came too late

In horror they heard
The rattle of gunfire
Tearing at chains
And thin flesh

Silent streets echo
Ghostlike footsteps
The air is still
Nothing moves
An empty can clatters
Across a path
A reminder.

Rain

The rain looked like melting silver
That soaked the soil
And became black
Leaking into every crack
Where seeds began to stir

Plump nubs of green
Push upwards
Reaching for light
Vulnerable
With nowhere to hide
Until
Petals open helplessly wide
A celebration of colour
In a bleak world

Part 3

Sleepless

She sat on the edge of the bed
And swayed slightly
Like a ghost debating
Whether to vanish
Or not

The night had been long and sleepless
Sitting there in the shadow of a shadow
She waited
For the sun to rise
And banish the darkness

Silence drifted around her
Like a balloon losing helium and
She stared through the window
At the almost silent city

A thin trickle of traffic
Lighting the veins
Of a dark dusk.

She anticipated the moan of car horns
And sirens
Vehicles lining the ribbon of road
Like slow moving beetles

And she knew
That as daylight took hold
She would need to sleep.

Play

The old man watches quietly as
Children play
And feed on happiness

They eat it greedily as
Dreams are captured
And re dreamed

The old man listens as
The trees whisper and watch

Time becomes elastic and
Birdsong pierces the air

Like love.

Tomorrow

Tomorrow
Where the black gulls fly
Red in beak
In claw
And eye
Eternal
As the deep blue sky
Seething power and light

The day proves strong
Alive and
Long
Sounding out
Belated song
For all the yesterdays
Now gone
Forever
Out of sight.

Silent Fugue

Streams of light
Through another door
Open to the evening
Once more

Watch the aftermath
Of the present earth
To each new mind
Ever giving birth
A seed of thought
A monologue of fear
For the darkness foreseen
Now drawing near

The choice of an age
Of serenity parts
With a feeling of hope
Reaching their hearts

The Couple

They walked down the path
Arm in arm
He was hunched over and
Had a face like a knot

She was hanging off his every word
As always
How absurd
His sentences were punctuated with
Rasping vocals
He sounded as though he'd started smoking
In the womb

I'm old
I suppose
He said as
Raindrops glistened
On the end of his bulbous nose
And this is my wife
Been with her for most of my life

She smiled and
Her lipstick mouth slipped slightly
Off centre

She wore a short sleeved
Sequined dress
Old loose skin
Hung off thin arms
Like chewing gum
Her words came tumbling fast
Slipping out like drool

This unlikely couple who maybe
Arrived in a timeslip
Don't fit with the modern world
But they litter the streets
Amongst others they meet
And point at their nemesis like freaks
Pointing at a circus

But we must forgive
This world in which we live
For there but for the freaks
Go I.

Only a Child Could Dream

The scene was extraordinary
A silent river rippled
A child gazed across the expanse
At moon polished water
Entranced

The moment was infused with
Imaginary wonderings
Fragile yet strong
Where only innocence could belong

Another world opened up
With dreams undreamed.
Where memories sat waiting
To be made
And the air was needing
To be breathed

Where only a child could dream.

www.ingramcontent.com/pod-product-compliance
Lightning Source LLC
Chambersburg PA
CBHW052037070526
44584CB00020B/3144